LESSONS FROM HEAVEN

PAIGE WILLIAMS

Lessons from Heaven

Paige Michael Williams

Copyright © 2023

Published by Seraph Creative in 2023

United States / United Kingdom / South Africa / Australia

www.seraphcreative.org

ISBN 978-1-958997-33-8

CONTENTS

Foreword   5

Introduction   7

Who is the Holy Spirit   9

One: What Is In The World?   15

Two: His House (Temple)   18

Three: The Principle of Remembrance   21

Four: The Purpose of The Wilderness   24

Five: The Falling Away   26

Six: Sons Of Perdition   29

Seven: Mistakes   32

Eight: Eternal Love Perspective   35

Nine: The Baptism of Suffering   37

Ten: The Repentance Covering   40

Eleven: The Word Covering   42

Twelve: The Seven Spirits of God   45

Thirteen: The Gifts of the Spirit   48

Fourteen: The Gathering   53

Conclusion   59

About the Author   61

FOREWORD

As I sat on my couch one morning with my journal open before me. Feeling spiritually stuffed or cramped up if you will. Like it was getting crowded within my own spirit. I really felt the urge to pour and to give what had been given and downloaded into me, and not to be a spiritual hoarder. As I was contemplating what I was supposed to do with all of the lessons and revelations the Holy Spirit had given me in my personal time with Him. That's when I heard *"Write a book."* So I embarked on a journey with God to compile lessons from my journals that He was emphasizing to me at the time, and the order in which they should be presented. This book is the result of that fellowship with The Spirit. May it bless you the way it has blessed me and more!

INTRODUCTION

This book is a series of personal lessons that The Holy Spirit taught me through the last few years of my life. I can personally say it was by His grace, mercy, and long-suffering that I have been able to receive these messages (lessons). I have made many mistakes and had downfalls in my relationship with Him. It has been the lessons I learned from these downfalls and mistakes that I have always been able to revisit and draw from. He is still teaching and empowering me to not only be able to hear, write, and deliver these lessons but to live them. Many of these lessons are His heart revealed in and through scripture for me personally and for the Body of Christ at large. He took His time teaching and disciplining me to Himself. He taught me each lesson, and I was able to handle and absorb them. First for myself, then for others. I have experienced much chastisement over the past few years as a result of The Spirit teaching me these lessons. *"For unto whomsoever much is given, of him shall be much required: and to whom men have committed much, of him they will ask the more (Luke 12:48)."*

You see there is a great price in the revelations of The Spirit because the messages carry the saving power of God Almighty and the intimate revelation of His Person. The revelation of scripture and the jewels therein are of eternal value and they lead us from faith to faith *"For therein is the righteousness of God revealed from faith to faith..."(Romans 1:17).* The closer we get to the Lord the more He expects from us, and the more He expects us to act as He acts and to do as He does. But this is impossible if we are out of union with Him. If we as saints desire to be more like Jesus, we are required to listen to and follow His Spirit whom He gave us. *"Howbeit when he, the Spirit of truth, is come, he will guide you into all truth: for he shall not speak of himself; but whatsoever he shall hear, that shall he speak: and he will shew you things to come (St. John 16:13)."* When you are a Spirit-filled believer there is an intimate relationship that should be formed with the Holy Spirit. He hears God the Father and our Lord Jesus Christ and the things that they speak in Heaven and reveals them unto us his children and ser-vants. He also knows the heart of God the Father and Jesus Christ and reveals not only His Word but His heart to us as well. These are called the deep things of God in scripture *"But God hath revealed them unto us by his Spirit: for the Spirit searcheth all things, yea, the deep things of God. For what man knoweth the things of a man, save the spirit of man which is in him? Even so the things of God knoweth no man, but the Spirit of God. Now we have received, not the spirit of the world, but the spirit which is of God; that we might know the things that are freely given to us of God (1 Corinthians 2:10-12)."*

WHO IS THE HOLY SPIRIT?

I've learned a series of lessons on the Holy Spirit and who He is as a Person. These lessons can only begin to explain who this third Person of the Godhead is, as you and I will be forever learning of His greatness and glory. These lessons and revelations given to me about the Spirit of God were not all taught to me by The Spirit Himself, but also by The Lord Jesus Christ. *"... For he shall not speak of himself (St. John 16:13)"* When this scripture says He will not speak of Himself, it does not mean that He won't literally talk about or reveal Himself. It means that what He speaks He has heard the Father and the Lord Jesus say *first* and He relays the message and revelation to us. The whole revelation of God is hidden in the Person of the Holy Spirit, that's why it is impossible to know God without Him!

Now whenever the Holy Spirit is spoken of in the Word of God it is God the Father and The Lord Jesus Christ speaking of Him. They represent Him and He represents them, for *"There is no jealousy in the Godhead."* The Lord spoke that to me one morning as I had been struggling in my mind about the Godhead and striving to give all of them glory and not depriving one person of the Godhead. But what He taught me was that the Godhead was glorified in all three Persons. God the Father, God the Son, and God the Spirit are all glorified because they are all equally God! The Holy Ghost spoke to me one afternoon as I was inquiring of Him about the Godhead and trying to understand them as God *together*. What

He said to me changed my life, he said, *"I AM GOD just as they (The Father and Jesus) are God, but I am my own Person, We love and respect one another's position and authority."* He continued, *"We are equal, but We manifest Glory differently."* This reveals that there is a relationship within the Godhead, they love and respect one another. The Father is not trying to be the Son (High Priest/Atonement/God in flesh), The Son is not trying to be the Holy Ghost (Guide/Endowment of Power) and vice versa. They are secure in who they are as God and in their position and authority in the Godhead...*Amazing!*

So, in my alone time with the Lord, He began to reveal to me just who the Holy Spirit is and who He (Jesus) is to me. The Word of God says that the Spirit is *another* Comforter (or companion) as Jesus was the original comforter to the disciples but now is seated at the right hand of The Father God. The Holy Spirit is given to us to be our companion and best friend. He was and is the precious promise of the Father that Jesus spoke of to His disciples. Our Lord Jesus expressed such urgency to depart from this earth to His disciples so that "The Comforter" would come. There is greater intimacy that is available through the Holy Ghost than it was with Jesus staying here in the flesh because He was limited to being in one place at one time. But through the Spirit He (Jesus) would be able to be with all of us at once which would result in the greater works that He spoke of in St. John chapter 14. We must understand that with each Person of the Godhead, there is another side or revelation of who God is.

One of the most eye-opening revelations I received about the Holy Spirit is that He was *everything* to Jesus while He was on earth. Jesus cherished the Spirit so much that He said there is no forgiveness for those who blaspheme (to speak against or evil of) Him **(St. Luke 12:10)**. In fact, it was through the Holy Ghost that Jesus was able to offer Himself on the cross. It was the Spirit that strengthened Him so that He could go through the torture, anguish, and pain of His crucifixion. But the Spirit didn't only strengthen Him to go to the cross, He kept Him perfect and blameless throughout His life, so that He could be our unblemished sacrifice. *"How much more shall the blood of Christ, who through the eternal Spirit offered himself without spot to God, purge your conscience from dead works to the living God?* **(Hebrews 9:14)**.

An often-unrealized mystery to the life of our Lord Jesus Christ is that He had the potential to sin. He was perfect in spirit being God, but He was made in the *likeness* of sinful flesh. That is why He is called in the Bible *the second Adam* or the second perfect man. And just like Adam in the garden, He was given the opportunity to be disobedient. This is why Satan tempted Him in the wilderness, He was trying to get Him to give in to the flesh and sin, thereby disqualifying Him as our Savior. He could not have been tempted if He did not have the potential to sin. The testimony of His perfection is more glorious in the fact that He had the choice to sin and chose to remain blameless! That's why He's a good High Priest, because He understands our daily struggles. He wasn't only acquainted with them on the cross, but every day of His life. He chose every day to yield Himself to the leadership and governing of the Holy Spirit and to do the will of the Father. You must understand that if Jesus had disobeyed the Spirit of God just *once,* the salvation of man was over! In order to be The Good and Faithful High Priest, He could not have been kept *from* temptation, but He had to be bombarded by it. He had to know through and through the pull, struggle, and battle with temptation. That's why the important part to realize is that He was led of the Spirit into the wilderness, to be tempted, and it's the same with us today. The Holy Ghost does not keep us from the hard or tough things in life. He allows us to go *through* them and to overcome them so that we can deliver others, just as Jesus did. You see, the Spirit had to perfect Jesus, this point is highlighted in Hebrews 5:8, ***"Though He were a Son, yet learned he obedience through the things which he suffered."***

We must understand that Jesus did not come to earth as God but as a man. He did nothing in His earthly ministry as Deity but as a man yielded and empowered by the Spirit of God. He is our example because everything He did, He did as a man by the power of the Holy Ghost. If He had done anything on the earth as God, He could not have been our example or our resurrection because He did it as Deity and not as a man! And we as a man wouldn't have been able to live through Him and be partakers of His Resurrection Life because He acted as God, and God is above the earthly realm and has all power, which man *did not!* That's another example of why He is called the second Adam because He operated in perfection as a *Man; and not as God.* It's the very reason we are able to be made perfect because Jesus accomplished perfection in the flesh as a man, where the first Adam fell. Now we can do the same thing that Jesus did! But He was a man who completely submitted to the authority and power of the Holy Ghost (and we *must* follow His example to get His results).

In essence, The Holy Spirit operated as the Father to Jesus on earth, and rightfully so. It was the Holy Spirit that overshadowed Mary and created Jesus' body in her womb, and He fathered Jesus while He was on the Earth. St. Luke 1:35 expresses it this way, *"And the angel answered and said unto her, The Holy Ghost shall come upon thee, and the power of the Highest shall overshadow thee: therefore also that holy thing which shall be born of thee shall be called the Son of God."*

Jesus lived just as we lived, he had to grow in knowledge and stature as the scriptures states, He had to learn how to be who He was called to be from the beginning! He was personally taught by the Holy Spirit how to be the Son of God in flesh. As the Word tells us, *"For as many as are led by the Spirit of God, they are the sons of God* (**Romans 8:10**)." It was because of His obedience to the Holy Spirit that the Father was able to testify, *"This is my beloved Son, in whom I am well pleased* (**St. Matthew 3:17**).*"*

This is the same pattern that we must follow in order to please the Father. Submission to the Spirit will always produce mighty sons of God. This is why Jesus was so emphatic about going back to the Father, so that He could send the Holy Spirit! He had come to the experiential knowledge that it was IMPOSSIBLE for man to be holy without the Holy Spirit. He knew that just as the Spirit created his body in the womb, men would need the Spirit to create them all over again! And not only did they need to be made over by the Spirit but filled with Him as well. We need Him on the inside of us, leading and guiding us, just as He did with our Lord. We need Him to comfort us in the most trying times of our lives, just as He did with Jesus in the Garden of Gethsemane, so that He (Jesus) could fulfill His Purpose. It is impossible to fulfill our purpose and destiny without the comforting of the Holy Spirit.

The Holy Spirit is not only our Comforter, but our nurturer, meaning He is responsible for raising us from babes in Christ to mature and seasoned believers or into Sonship. *"But as many as received him, to them gave the power to become the sons of God... (**St. John 1:12**)"* He is the Person of the Godhead that strives (labors) with us (humanity) desiring to bring us to the revelation of Jesus Christ in whom alone is salvation! It is the Holy Ghost that leads us to Jesus; He is the first Person of the Godhead that we meet in coming to salvation because only He can reveal the Lord

Jesus Christ to us so that we can receive Him. It is the Spirit that opens our eyes when the gospel is preached and moves sinners to repentance. It is of The Spirit that we are born again. As it is written, *"Verily, verily, I say unto thee, except a man be born of water and of the Spirit, he cannot enter into the kingdom of God. That which is born of the flesh is flesh; and that which born of the Spirit is spirit (St. John 3:5-6).*

When we come to repentance and faith in Christ Jesus, our old man (or spirit) dies and The Holy Spirit creates in us a new spirit that is after or like God, this work is called being born of the Spirit. It is our birth or entrance into the Spirit realm, just as a natural birth is the entrance into the physical realm. After we are born of the Spirit our desires change from earthly desires to spiritual desires. There is also another work of the Spirit called Spirit Baptism. *"I indeed baptize you with water unto repentance: but he that cometh after me is mightier than I, whose shoes I am not worthy to bear: he shall baptize you with the Holy Ghost, and with fire: (St. Matthew 3:11)."* It is Jesus Christ who baptizes believers in The Holy Ghost, once we repent and believe the gospel of Jesus Christ putting our faith in Him and His work on the cross; we become candidates for this precious promise of the Holy Spirit. *"...Upon whom thou shalt see the Spirit descending, and remaining on him, the same is he which baptizeth with the Holy Ghost (St. John 1:33)."* Acts 2:38-39 states, *"Then Peter said unto them, Repent, and be baptized every one of you in the name of Jesus Christ for the remission of sins, and ye shall receive the gift of the Holy Ghost. For the promise is unto you, and to your children, and to all that are afar off, even as many as the Lord our God shall call."* Spirit baptism or the infilling of the Spirit is the greatest gift that we have received as a result of the atoning blood of Jesus Christ, apart from salvation itself. When we are born of the Spirit, we become new creatures or new beings, and the Holy Spirit is with us (**St. John 14:17**), and when we're baptized in water we have put on Christ (**Galatians 3:27**). But when we are baptized or filled with the Holy Spirit, He dwells within us and unifies Himself with our spirit. It is in the work of being baptized or filled with the Spirit that we now become His dwelling place or His temple. And this glorious outpouring of the Spirit will be signified by speaking in other tongues (**Acts 2:4**).

The Holy Spirit is also our seal or stamp from God that we belong to Him! He seals our salvation, which we receive through repentance and faith in

Christ Jesus. The best example I can give is when in biblical times they used seals on their letters to authenticate the message. It is the same with us according to scripture. We are epistles of Christ, which are read of all men, and we have the seal of God almighty upon us to authenticate us as valued or authentic messages (messengers) from Him to humanity. The New Oxford Dictionary defines a seal as *a device or substance that is used to join two things together so as to prevent them from coming apart or prevent anything from passing between them.* The Spirit is our seal that keeps us connected with God and He also keeps anything from coming between us and The Father. Wow!

"In whom ye also trusted, after that ye heard the word of truth, the gospel of your salvation: in whom also after ye believed, ye were sealed with that holy Spirit of Promise, Which is the earnest of our inheritance until the redemption of the purchased possession, unto the praise of his glory (Ephesians 1:13-14)."

The Spirit is also our source of power (Dunamis). *"But ye shall receive power, after that the Holy Ghost is come upon you: and ye shall be witnesses and in all Judaea, and in Samaria, and unto the uttermost part of the earth."* The Holy Spirit Himself is the power of every believer just as He was the power manifested in our Lord Jesus Christ. As Jesus said the servant is not greater than his lord so as the Spirit was Jesus' power in the earth, so He is ours. Even the gifts of the Spirit listed in 1 Corinthians 12, they represent the supernatural power of the Holy Spirit. The gifts of the Holy Spirit are NOT natural gifts they are supernatural manifestations of God's power through human vessels. These gifts and the power of The Holy Ghost are given for the purpose of spiritual warfare and for the perfection of the Church, and for signs and wonders to unbelievers. These are just a few operations of The Holy Spirit in our daily lives.

LESSON ONE: WHAT IS IN THE WORLD?

There are three references to the word *world* in the Bible. One refers to the physical world of the Earth (land, sea, animals etc...) *"...I will utter things which have been kept secret from the foundation of the world (Matthew 13:35)"*, the second refers to humanity (people, human beings) *"For God so loved the world that He gave His only begotten Son...(John 3:16)"*, and the third and most spiritually unrecognized is the spiritual kingdom of darkness *"Love not the world neither the things that are in the world. If any man love the world, the love of the Father is not in him" (1 John 2:15).* Here we see that there is a spiritual kingdom of darkness that dwells here on earth, Jesus said, *"If ye were of the world, the world would love his own: but because ye are not of the world, but I have chosen you out of the world therefore the world hateth you" (John 15:19).*

We in the physical realm do not see a kingdom built as we do natural kingdoms of the world, this is a spiritual kingdom in the spirit realm that at this present time, is controlling the majority of humanity. We in the natural realm only see the manifestation of the works of the spiritual realm. For example, we may not see the person of the Holy Spirit manifest and move upon individuals, but we in the natural see the joy, tears, praise, and worship that comes as a result of what has first taken place in the spirit realm. It is the same on the opposing end, we do not physically see demon spirits enter the souls of humanity, however, in the natural, we see the manifestation of what has taken place: rage, lustfulness, hate and perversion. These things are a result of the kingdom of darkness ruling in the hearts and minds of those alive on earth.

When our Lord Jesus Christ was tempted by Satan in the wilderness He was tempted in three areas, these areas are the same three temptations that He uses to tempt all of humanity to this very day. The scripture states, *"For all that is in the world, the lust of the flesh, and the lust of the eyes, and the pride of life, is not of the Father, but is of the world" (1 John 2:16).* It is in these three areas that all of humanity has been tested and tempted since the world began. Jesus states in the book Revelation several times *"to him that overcometh..."* and these three traps of the world are what we must overcome.

Some in the faith have overcome the lust of the flesh yet struggle with the lust of the eyes and the pride of life, and we can see the other scenarios that could play out within these traps of the world. But God is calling for a people without spots or wrinkles or any such thing, which shows that he desires us to overcome in all three of these areas. An example of someone overcoming two areas but still being entrapped in one is the story of the rich young ruler in St. Luke 18.

In this event, a young wealthy man approached Christ inquiring what he must do to inherit eternal life, and Jesus listed the commandments. His reply was that he had kept the commandments from his youth up, but Jesus knew that the pride of life abided within his heart, so to expose his heart's true condition He told him to sell all he had and follow him! But the young ruler could not let go of his riches, though he was not overcome with the lust of the flesh or the lust of the eyes, the pride of life had gripped his heart and forced him to leave that encounter with Jesus, empty. He couldn't let go of his lifestyle, which he felt entitled to because he was entrapped in "the pride of life", and because of that, he could not forsake his lifestyle to follow the Lord.

This is the state of many in the church that *think* they are true disciples and are not, even if they're keeping the Ten Commandments like the rich young ruler. If we have anything in our lives that we cannot forsake to follow or serve the Lord then we are not true disciples, and if you're not a true disciple then you are not really following Christ. Which means many in the Church are in deception. Deceived into thinking that they are true disciples, following Jesus, and are in good standing with God, but it is not so. That's why in the first three chapters of Revelation Jesus addressed the seven churches in Asia Minor. To make them aware of their true condition whether good or bad in relation to Him. It is the heart of Jesus that we all walk in the light, and to walk in the light is to walk in the truth.

As most of us know, the truth is not always easy to hear or to tell but it is best, and it is the truth that makes us free from the darkness. When we overcome the world (these three areas) we are then liberated and able to be used by God in an extraordinary way! As long as we are overcome or defeated in one or more of these areas God's hand is limited on how much He can pour into us, especially before His people. Great damage and devastation can potentially be done to the body of Christ if He would exalt you before you have overcome (the world), for the simple reason that you are still bound in one or more of these areas. God can no longer afford for His leaders and shepherds to publicly be overcome by sin because it hurts the message of Christ to a dying world. His messengers are publicly tainted and bound by the same strongholds as the unbelievers that they are preaching liberty to, and we as the messengers of God have to understand that we are representatives of God's choice, meaning we have the ability to lift Him up and to tear Him down before humanity by our lives. We must be overcomers of the *world* to fulfill our purpose and the high call of God in Christ Jesus!

LESSON TWO: HIS HOUSE (TEMPLE)

As most saints know, we are the temple of the Holy Ghost, but many of us carry this revelation carelessly. We carry this spiritual information in the back of our minds. If we always had this in the forefront of our hearts and minds, we as the temples of God would walk very differently. There are two scriptures that the Holy Spirit used to illustrate two very important and relevant truths in the church today. The first is *St. Matthew 21:1-17* in this scripture Jesus is entering into the temple in Jerusalem. As He enters the holy city on the back of a donkey the people hail Him as King, and they praise Him calling Him Hosanna. *"And the multitudes that went before, and that followed, cried, saying, Hosanna to the Son of David: Blessed is he that cometh in the name of the Lord; Hosanna in the highest (Matthew 21:9)."*

This to the naked eye looks great, but if you keep reading the scripture you will find out that the same people who were praising and hailing Him as King, would turn around and proclaim "crucify Him" just a few days later! This exemplifies the heart of Jesus. He will endure with those whom He knows will eventually betray and turn on Him (Judas/people of Jerusalem). What a faithful friend! However, because He knew their hearts, He could not commit (bind) Himself to them. He was willing to receive the praise of those outside of His house even knowing their hearts. We could use this scenario to represent the world (people/unsaved humanity) who do not have a personal relationship with Jesus, those who have only known Him by the hearing of the ear. This point is represented in these verses, *"And when he was come into Jerusalem, all the city was moved, saying, Who is this? And the multitude said, This is Jesus the prophet of Nazareth of Galilee (St. Matthew 21:10-11)."* They would be the ones outside of the temple praising Him. But as the Lord continues His journey to enter into His Father's House, we see a different reaction.

The Bible states, *"And Jesus went into the temple of God, and cast out all them that sold and bought in the temple, and overthrew the tables of the money changers, and the seats of them that sold doves, And said unto them, It is written, My house shall be called the house of prayer, but ye have made it a den of thieves (St. Matthew 21:12-13)."* The things that went on outside of the House of God, the people who didn't know Jesus who would eventually betray Him He endured them BUT those who were within the house of God, who were supposed to know the Father and have a relationship with Him made this mistake and He overthrew them! Wow! Their mistake was that they TOOK/STOLE the focus off of God and made it about themselves, making the house of God into a den of thieves. They stole from the glory of God Almighty, distracting the people from their original purpose, which was to come and fellowship through prayer, worship and to hear His Word. Many don't realize that they've partnered with Satan to steal, kill, and destroy the people of God, as well as sinners coming into the house of God Satan desires to steal the seed of the Word being sown into the lives of believers and sinners alike when they enter the House of God (St. Matthew 13:18-22). There is one thing he understands that many people on earth do not, and that is the principle of harvest, better known as: sowing and reaping. One thing the enemy fights so hard to accomplish on Earth is to keep the seed (Word) from falling on good ground (Right Hearts). So, he will pull all the stops to keep the Word of God, both written and Rhema, from taking root in the hearts of men. He knows if it does it will eventually bring forth a harvest and bear much fruit. This was his objective then and it is the same in the House of God today. There are many people that are coming into the Church to pray, worship, and hear a Word from God, but when they arrive, they are distracted by so many other things (what people are wearing, people's faces, attitudes, gossip, cell phones, social media/texting, and unfruitful conversation.)

These things cause us to become a den of thieves within the Church. When we as Christians allow ourselves to be distracted by these things, or even worse, distract others from their original purpose for coming, we make ourselves thieves in the house of God. We allow Satan to use these things to take away our worship and prayer to God, as well as our attention to the preached Word of God, and we allow them to become stumbling blocks in the lives of other believers so that they never make it into the true temple of God (Spirit Realm). We must understand that there is harsher punishment and chastisement upon those who know God and do wrong, than those who don't know Him and do wrong, ESPECIALLY in His house.

LESSON THREE: THE PRINCIPLE OF REMEMBRANCE

There is a principle The Lord, recently spoke and settled in my spirit. It's the principle of remembrance. Many Christians go through life with many questions. We ask questions as to why certain things happen in our lives and why God allows them to continue. We form opinions and reasoning as to why these things or events have taken place whether in the past or present. Sometimes we even make excuses for God because the conclusion we've come to leaves us viewing God in a negative light. So, in order to see God in a positive light we make unbiblical excuses for the Lord and His sovereignty. When in all actuality we feel that the Lord has made a mistake, or that He is insensitive, or that He just flat out doesn't care! So many times, we as believers seek the Lord for answers to questions we have in our hearts and minds, and we are thrown for a loop when we don't receive an answer but silence instead. It is because of the principle of remembrance, the scripture read in 2 Timothy 2:15 *" Study to shew thyself approved unto God, a workman that needeth not to be ashamed, rightly dividing the word of truth."*

The word of God tells us clearly to STUDY to show ourselves approved to GOD, so that we can RIGHTLY DIVIDE the word of truth, and not be ashamed. Often times we are made ashamed before the Lord without knowing it because we fail to study His Word and we've become lazy

Christians or lazy WORKMEN over His Word and in times when we need the Word, we don't have it in us to guide us. In St. John 14:26 it says, *"But the Comforter, which is the Holy Ghost, whom the Father will send in my name, he shall teach you all things, and bring all things to your remembrance, whatsoever I have said unto you."*

So, you see the Holy Ghost is sent to bring all things back to memory whatsoever the Lord has spoken to us. Now the Lord will speak to us and give us a personal word, something that is not in or cannot be read in scripture, such as "Go and witness to that young lady standing on the corner", but there is much that the Lord wants to say to us through His written Word. And we can miss His voice many times because it is found in His Word and because we haven't been in the Word as we should be. The Spirit will only bring things back to our remembrance or memory that we have already heard from the Lord Jesus whether personally or in scripture. If we have not heard, we cannot receive. Faith comes by hearing and hearing by the word of God.

It's not the Lord's responsibility to tell or reveal things to us things that we could so easily pick up and read in scripture, and He will not reward laziness. So, I encourage every saint, even myself, to study the Word of God and to fill ourselves with Him so that in our times of need we will have spirits full of The Word. Words that will be readily brought back to our remembrance by the Holy Ghost!

There is a two-fold principle of remembrance. The other principle is based on the foundation of gratefulness and thankfulness. Many times, as saints we can unknowingly become spoiled, we want God (An Emperor) to move when and how we want Him to, and to be at our beckon and call. He often times in His grace and mercy, does bless and rescue us, but we become so used to His instant provision and blessing that we can belittle all that He has done, always asking and wanting the next thing. But what God will do is allow a season of remembrance for His people, by not being as busy in our lives. He does this out of love so that we can truly become thankful and appreciate all that He has *already* done for us and *remember* His goodness and wonderful works.

You see, He's a good Father, so He's determined to bring the best out of His children. So, He must teach them to have a heart of remembrance, which is a heart of reverence!

LESSON FOUR: THE PURPOSE OF THE WILDERNESS

Many of us know the story in the Bible where Jesus was baptized in the river Jordan by John the Baptist. During His baptism, the Holy Spirit descended upon Him, and the Father spoke from heaven declaring, ***"This is my beloved Son in whom I am well pleased" (St. Matthew 3:17).*** This was a glorious manifestation of God among the people and was a representation of water baptism and Spirit baptism. Jesus was submerged in water (water baptism) and the Spirit descended upon Him and abided as a picture of Spirit baptism, as well as a picture of the anointing of God resting upon Him. But it's what happened next that many believers fail to correlate to our own lives as Jesus is our example!

The scripture states that He was driven by The Spirit into the wilderness and tempted by the devil. If Jesus is our example, then that means this is the same process that the Holy Ghost leads us through as well. We are excited and on fire and zealous for the Lord after we receive salvation and Spirit baptism, but we do not prepare our hearts for the wilderness. The truth is we must learn how to overcome and thrive in the wilderness in order to be ready for true ministry.

The wilderness is meant to: teach us dependence on the Holy Spirit, develop closeness with Him through trial, tribulation, and temptation, and also to teach you the reality of The Spirit within you. It is a process of developing our character or the fruit of the Spirit within our lives. One thing we must also notice is that Jesus and the Holy Spirit were not alone in the wilderness but the scriptures state that Satan was there also to tempt Jesus. He used the three things that are in the world that we discussed previously in Lesson One *(1 John 2:16)* to tempt The Lord, and The Lord overcame him! And it is the same with us, we must overcome Satan's temptations in the wilderness in order to operate in the manifest power of God in ministry. It is the power that God gives to the overcomer, those who learn how to thrive in the wilderness! This is why Jesus proclaimed that there was not a greater man born of a woman than John the Baptist because he learned how to thrive in the wilderness, and many lives were changed because of it.

There is a scripture in St. John 7:38-39, *"He that believeth on me, as the scripture has said, out of his belly shall flow rivers of living water (But this spake he of the Spirit, which they that believe on him should receive: for the Holy Ghost was not yet given, because that Jesus was not yet glorified."* Now everyone knows that if someone is left in the wilderness for an extended period of time without food or water they will die. That is exactly why we need the living water which is the Holy Ghost! He is the one that sustains us in this life (wilderness) until we return home (Paradise). But paradise is exactly what He creates on the inside of us, just as He did at the beginning of creation. The Spirit of God is literally our Life in this world, and we will spiritually die without Him! We as saints are to literally become trees of life in the wilderness of this world that others may come and draw from. God wants us to become life-givers in the wilderness bearing much fruit, not those barely surviving or at the point of death. Those who can *thrive* in the wilderness seasons of their life will *always* come out with greater power and authority!

LESSON FIVE: THE FALLING AWAY

I strongly believe we are seeing the manifestation of this prophecy in scripture. There are two main verses in scripture that attest to this reality in the last days (our days) of a great falling away. The first one I want to emphasize is 1 Timothy 4:1-2, ***"Now the Spirit speaketh expressly, that in the latter times some shall depart from the faith, giving heed to seducing spirits, and doctrines of devils; Speaking lies in hypocrisy; and having their conscience seared with a hot iron."***

Most saints have the perception that this falling away will result in many leaving the churches and no longer attending services. But that is not what The Holy Ghost is expressing through the Apostle Paul in his letter to Timothy. What he's speaking of is a last day departure from the ***faith.*** That means that churches will still be full, that men, women, and children will still be attending services, but in their hearts and minds they have departed from the faith (Truth). The Scripture says giving heed to seducing spirits. Now when speaking of seducing spirits, we are not just talking about spirits of lust and perversion, but any spirit that leads a believer from the truth. The transliterated word for *seducing* is *planos,* which means an impostor or misleader, deceiver seducing. There are many ways in which believers are being deceived in these last days, but the sad part of this scripture is that they are giving heed or listening to these spirits. That means that men and women in the body of Christ are giving space to the devil and his evil spirits, and consequently are being led astray!

The Bible clearly states in James 4:7, *"Submit yourselves therefore to God. Resist the devil, and he will flee from you."* So, if Satan or these seducing spirits aren't fleeing from you, that means you are not resisting them. The only way to properly resist them is by using The Word of God (our Sword) to combat them. That's how our Lord Jesus Christ overcame Satan in the wilderness, by using His Word against him. Evil spirits can only stay where there is space or a place for them (*Ephesians 4:27*). And where there is a listening ear please believe me, Satan and his evil spirits are more than willing to deceive...ask Eve.

Now the next part of the verse is equally as important. It says *and doctrines of devils.* So, some in the church will not only be giving heed to seducing spirits, but to doctrines or teachings of devils. Now one may ask the question "How can saints be deceived like this?" Good question! The answer is found in 2 Timothy 4:3-4, *"For the time will come when they will not endure sound doctrine; but after their own lusts shall they heap to themselves teachers, having itching ears, and they shall turn away their ears from the truth, and shall be turned unto fables."*

You see, people will not want to endure sound doctrine, meaning they will not sit under the Truth of God's Word to the perfecting of their souls. All of God's Word does not *feel good,* it's often used for edification (building up), encouragement, and comfort. But as The Word says it is also useful for reproof, correction, and rebuke; these are the parts of God's Word that people in our time do not want to hear, sit through, and receive or as the scripture says, *"endure".* But what we often fail to understand is that God would not be a good Father if He did not correct or chastise us! We need His chastisement and correction so that we can grow and mature in Him and serve Him more perfectly. It's just like when good earthly parents correct us when we're wrong, so that we will not go in that direction, but will once again take or get back on the right path, and it's the same with God.

The Bible tells us to *endure chastening, and God dealeth with you as with sons* (Hebrews 12:7), if we are to be the sons and daughters of God (which includes His Inheritance) we must endure chastening. We are not only supposed to endure chastening but, *"My Son despise not thou the chastening of the Lord, nor faint when thou art rebuked of him. For whom the Lord loveth he chasteneth, and scourgeth every son whom he recieveth*

(Hebrews 12:5-6)." To despise something is to think little or nothing of it. The Scripture is in other words telling us to highly value His chastening because His chastening brings us to bountiful righteousness which means bearing much fruit. And Jesus said in St. John 15:2 & 4, *"Every branch in me that beareth not fruit he taketh away: and every branch that beareth fruit, he purgeth it, that it may bring forth more fruit. Abide in me and I in you. As the branch cannot bear fruit of itself, except it abide in the vine; no more can ye, except ye abide in me."* The key is to abide in Him which would naturally include enduring chastisement and being purged as the Scripture states so that you can bear more fruit or in other words be more profitable to the Kingdom of God.

LESSON SIX:
SONS OF PERDITION

In St. John 17:12 Jesus makes a monumental statement that I'm sure many have overlooked as I myself did for years, until the Holy Spirit highlighted this point to me. It reads, *"...those that thou gavest me I have kept, and none of them is lost, but the son of perdition; that the scripture might be fulfilled."* If you look up the Strong's dictionary definition of perdition it is defined as a person of ruin or loss, perishing and damnable (awaiting destruction). That being said, in the context of the scripture Jesus was speaking of Judas Iscariot who would betray Him. But why was he called the son of perdition? If he is the son of perdition, there must be a father of perdition.

Now if we highlight the qualities of perdition: loss, ruin, and destruction, we can take a deeper look into what Jesus was really saying. The father of perdition is Satan. Why? Satan was once in heaven before the throne of God, a guardian of the presence of God, but he decided to turn his affection and love from the One True God to himself and was utterly cast out of the Kingdom of Heaven! So by definition, Satan experienced a *loss* of place or position with God, was placed in a state of spiritual *ruin* (losing the glory God had given him), and is now awaiting his appointed time of *destruction.* He fits the definition of perdition perfectly. Judas the son of perdition was called to be an Apostle of Jesus Christ, he healed the sick and cast out devils with the seventy Jesus sent out two by two, yet before it was all said and done his heart had turned away from Jesus and he ultimately suffered the *loss* of his place, position, and salvation. The Bible even goes as far as to say in St. Luke 10:20 that his name was written in Heaven, that means that it had to be blotted out (Revelations 3:5). He then became a man in spiritual *ruin (torn down, devastated),* which ultimately lead to his suicide; which brought him to his *destruction* or his spirit being cast into hell for eternity.

The sad truth is that there are and will be many more sons of perdition. Those who start out in the faith or with God but then forsake Him, leaving the faith and forfeiting their position and salvation with God. I know this contradicts the common belief *once saved, always saved* but that is not a scriptural fact for all, the scriptures clearly state in 1 Timothy 4:1, *"Now the Spirit speaketh expressly, that in the latter times some shall depart from the faith, giving heed to seducing spirits, and doctrines of devils."* That means that some who start in the faith will at some point and time leave the faith and walk away from Jesus Christ. The Bible also states that there would be a *falling away* before the day of Christ in 2 Thessalonians 2:3. As Jesus said in St. John 17:12, he had kept all that the Father had given Him, except the son of perdition and it is the same today.

Jesus keeps all the Father gives Him, *except or save* the son(s) of perdition! The Spirit of God will not endure sons of perdition; if any man desires to leave or forsake Him he will grievingly let them. To stay with the Lord must be a choice, He will not force or make anyone serve or stay with Him no matter how much He loves them. In Hebrews 12:39 the scripture states, *"But we are not of them that draw back unto perdition; but of them that believe to the saving of the soul."* This scripture is an eye-opener, because it shines a light on the fact that there are people in the church that will *draw back* unto perdition. When I read this verse, I picture someone pulling away from The Holy Spirit, the Spirit releasing them and the person backing up to the point of no return. A person must begin to draw back or go backwards pulling away from the Spirit and Love of God, then continue on that backward path until they cross the line reaching the point of perdition. The truth is: *You can go too far!* Now I must say for a person that falls into sin or backslides there is hope and its *repentance.* Repentance is us running back into the arms of God, acknowledging that we were wrong and allowing Him to clean us and lead us in the right direction. Perdition *only comes* to those who continue to draw back and do not return as the prodigal son in St. Luke 15:20-24.

In 2 Peter 3:7 we read, *"But the heavens and the earth which are now, by the same word are kept in store, reserved unto fire against the day of judgement and perdition of ungodly men."* The final state of perdition is destruction. All those who have fallen in perdition are literally in the same state as the devil and his fallen angels; which are awaiting destruction.

LESSON SEVEN: MISTAKES

One afternoon while meditating on the Lord, The Spirit spoke a word to me that forever changed my life! He said, *"You're going to make mistakes but I love you anyway. You are going to need the mistakes to learn the lessons that I need you to learn to become the man I need you to be."* You see, growing up in Holiness (Pentecostal/Apostolic), mistakes were not associated with God or our relationship with Him. It was something looked down upon and I adopted that mindset. When the Lord spoke this word to me, it threw me for a spiritual loop; because His perception of mistakes was not what I thought it was. He made His love clear to me that He loved me in spite of my mistakes and knowing that I would make them in the future. I found out that He uses our mistakes as a vital part of our purpose. There are things that we will never learn or that will be revealed to us outside of the lessons learned from mistakes.

Mistakes also create a sense of humility and dependence on the Holy Spirit to lead and guide us into all truth. They cause a loss of confidence in one-self and force the believer to put all of their confidence in Christ Jesus. Thus Proverbs 3:3, **"My son lean not to thine own understanding, in all thy ways acknowledge him and He will direct your path."** There were several key points and analogies the Holy Spirit gave to me; one being: *"Every mistake is not a sin."* He then gave me a financial analogy where He showed how we feel and see the effects of our financial mistakes after we've made them. Even how our bodies eventually see and feel the mistakes we made in our eating habits, and we learn from the reality of our condition. He also showed me how the disciples made many mistakes even though they were with Him and constantly in His Presence, but He used their mistakes to teach and give them wisdom for the future. Sometimes the Lord will allow a smaller mistake to take place in your life to teach you a lesson that will keep you from a bigger mistake down the line. That's part of the Amazing Grace that saves us! Because God is more concerned with how we finish than how we start, His design is to grow us up into Him through life experiences that help mold us into His Image and Likeness. Even He **"...learned obedience through the things which He suffered** (Hebrews 5:8)."

We as His servants are not greater than our Master. A valuable lesson I've learned is that just because we are close to The Lord does not mean we are in union with Him, because union with Him breeds perfection. We may be close to The Lord in our relationship with Him, but that in no wise means, we always see as He sees, hear as He hears, and think as He thinks. And it is our mistakes that oftentimes give us a clear picture of where we are and where He is! And just like the disciples, our mistakes can teach many, because mistakes are lessons made real. This brings me to the main point The Spirit made in this conversation; The School of Grace!

All true Christians are enrolled in the School of Grace, and just like school in the natural realm, we may receive bad grades in different courses every once in a while. Many Christians believe that they've failed when in reality they have only received a bad grade or low score. So consequently, many believers give up or drop out of the school of Grace. But naturally when we receive a low score, the teacher doesn't kick us out of school, we remain in the classroom. Only now, we have a better understanding of the area in which we are weak. And can therefore give that area the required attention it deserves so we may improve; so, it is in the School of Grace. But in balance, if we continually get low scores we can't pass! We will fail, and we will be forced to repeat the same courses. We must give the effort that is required to stay in the School of Grace. Consistent bad grades show carelessness and a lack of study for the coursework. It reveals who isn't paying attention. 2 Timothy 2:15 states, **"*Study to shew thyself approved unto God, a workman that needeth not to be ashamed, rightly dividing the word of truth.*"** But there is a way that is much worse, in which many believers fail...that is PRIDE. Because of pride, many believers don't ask for the help they need. They refuse to humble themselves before their fellow classmates (saints) and as a result they never get the help they desperately need. In the School of Grace, the humble receive additional grace **(James 4:6)**. It is the student's or disciple's hunger to succeed at all costs, even at the cost of their own ego; that will give their soul the true success they desire. Success in *the Spirit!*

LESSON EIGHT: ETERNAL LOVE PERSPECTIVE

As the last day Saints, it is essential that we have an eternal love perspective. You may ask "What is an eternal love perspective?" Glad you asked! It is the spiritual insight and grace to love humanity through a God perspective. We view love very differently from The Lord. We love selfishly for our own benefit to preserve what we desire from people. But God loves from a selfless perspective for the benefit of the other person, especially their eternal benefit. He commands us as His disciples in St. John 15:12, ***"This is my commandment, that ye love one another, as I have loved you."*** This means that we are not to love one another as we see fit, but as Christ has loved us; and oh, how He loves us!

What He really meant when He gave this commandment was for us to love from the perspective of eternity and not from an earthly perspective. For example, if we were to see someone, we're close to us willingly committing sin, it is our nature to turn a blind eye thinking that we are helping our relationship with them by not confronting them. We actually see it as loving them by not confronting them, holding them accountable or hurting their feelings; and in turn preserving our relationship from any forms of conflict (self-centeredness). Instead of loving their soul enough to try and keep them from eternal separation from God in hell; we'll often pacify them. This is NOT love; it is actually a form of hatred. We are to love as Christ loves, and Christ tells the truth even when it hurts. He is genuinely concerned about our eternal destination, and this is also the responsibility and call of his people.

1 Corinthians 13:6 (NIV) says, ***"Love does not delight in evil but rejoices with the truth."*** So, if we really love others, we'll tell them the truth regardless of how it affects our relationship with them in the here and now, because we have a bigger perspective. In all actuality if that person dies and goes to hell and we were around them on a consistent basis and never told them the truth in love; their blood is on our hands and God will judge us for that **(Ezekiel 33:6)**. We need to have a perspective that is set on seeing them enter into the kingdom of heaven for eternity. Trust me any relationship that was lost because of the love of the truth, granted, that person later heeds the truth you told them in love, you'll have all of eternity in heaven to rejoice with them!

LESSON NINE: THE BAPTISM OF SUFFERING

I was sitting in a Sunday service and my Pastor, Elder James E. Sanders was ministering the word of God. As I was listening to the sermon and looking at the scripture, he was reading the Holy Ghost and highlighted something to me. We were reading Hebrew 6:1-2 which read, *"Therefore leaving the principles of the doctrine of Christ, let us go on unto perfection, not laying again the foundation of repentance from dead works, and of faith toward God, OF THE DOCTRINE OF BAPTISMS, and of laying on of hands, and of the resurrection of the dead, and of eternal judgement.*

I had recently read St. Matthew 20:22-23 where the mother of a couple of the disciples had asked the Lord Jesus to allow her sons to sit with Him in His kingdom, one on His right and the other on His left. But Jesus told her that she didn't understand what she was asking! And He asked her sons a question saying *"... Are ye able to drink of the cup that I shall drink of, and to be baptized with the baptism that I am baptized with?* What was the baptism he was speaking of? It was the baptism of suffering. In St. Luke 12:50 (NLT) it reads this way *"I have a terrible baptism of suffering ahead of me, and I am under a heavy burden until it is accomplished."*

In Hebrew 6:1-2 the Spirit lets us know that the doctrine of baptisms is a foundation principle, meaning this is to be taught to new-Christians or babes in Christ! It is to be engrained and settled in the hearts of new disciples giving them proper edification for suffering. But this is not the case in the majority of the Western church; Jesus is sold to us as a solver of all of our problems and a heavenly genie to grant all of our wishes. But many do not realize that they have not become true disciples, for the simple fact that they have not given up (died) their own lives to allow Christ to live in and through them. They haven't accepted the call to true discipleship, which is death, discipline, and suffering. Jesus is calling us to deny ourselves, pick up our cross and follow Him. The scripture says in 2 Timothy 2:11-12, *"It is a faithful saying: For if we are dead with him, we shall also live with him: If we suffer, we shall also reign with him if we deny him, he also will deny us..."* He is actually calling us to die to ourselves, our will, and selfish ambitions. He wants people who are purely devoted to Him. As the scripture states we will not live with Him if we do not first die to ourselves, even as He did on the cross. It also says that we will not reign with him if we do not *suffer!*

With God, there is no glory without suffering. Suffering on the behalf of another is the greatest sign of love, and love that is not tested is not love at all. Just as we are submerged in water baptism, we have to allow God to fully submerge us into the baptism of suffering. The Bible says it is His good pleasure to try us until the end; this is because it purifies us and shows forth His glory. We are actually purified through suffering! The Bible also refers to suffering as the fire through which we must pass to enter gloriously into the kingdom. To enter gloriously into the kingdom of heaven we must receive all baptisms from God: the baptism of *repentance, water* baptism, *Spirit* baptism, *fire* baptism, baptism of *love* and the baptism of *suffering.* The early church rejoiced in their suffering because they were counted worthy by God to suffer for His sake. To be martyred for Christ-sake is actually the greatest honor in Heaven! But how many in the body of Christ have the ambition to be a martyr for Christ? We must first be spiritual martyrs, in order to be effective enough witnesses to be a physical martyr. Anyone worth dying for is worth living for; even if it is a life of suffering. And the consolation is that in your suffering you are not without The Comforter!

LESSON TEN: THE REPENTANCE COVERING

As I was spending my morning time with the Lord, the Spirit began to explain to me what was coming in the very near future, even in our present day. He explained to me that there will be demonic spirits released in this generation that had not been released in any other generation. And that many stands in the same position as ancient Egypt in the time of Moses, when the angel of death was to soon descend on them...uncovered!

Many people for many different reasons refuse to repent, just as the pharaoh did in the days of Moses. Two *main* reasons for a lack of repentance are *Pride* and *Deception*. In pride: thinking that we are better or in a better condition than we really are; and deception: believing that we see perfectly when we're blind. Pride will keep men from seeing their desperate need for the blood of Christ and the cross of Christ, as well as deception. Deception will also deceive many into believing that they are saved when they are actually in danger of hell's fire!

These two things among others are in direct contrast to *confession* which is a crucial part of repentance. To acknowledge our sins is the first step in repentance. If we never see ourselves as wrong or in sin, we will never truly desire a Savior. To acknowledge our sin and need for forgiveness is actually wisdom, and it will move us to take the necessary actions to be restored and *covered!* On the night that the angel of death descended upon the land of

Egypt only those who had the *blood covering* were spared or passed over. Even so, it shall be in the last days. Only those who have covered their houses (temple/body) with the blood of Christ applied from true repentance will be spared from the wrath of God coming on the nations. Only those who have the blood of Jesus on their door post will be covered, without the blood we are spiritually open to all sorts of demonic activity in our lives, as well as the wrath of God! The enemy can't pass through the blood of Jesus Christ, it's our protection. It keeps Satan from infiltrating our homes both spiritually and naturally. But more importantly, the blood of Christ grants us access to the Father God, which is the reason Jesus went to the Cross; to reconcile man to God (A restoration of intimate relationship and fellowship)!

The scripture says, *"...and without the shedding of blood there is no remission* (**Hebrews 9:22**)." Remission is defined by *Thayer's Definition* as a release from bondage or imprisonment; it's also defined by *Strong's definition* as freedom, pardon, deliverance, forgiveness and liberty. Whatever definition we emphasize, each one is something we need; and what we need only comes through *repentance!* Repentance is the change of heart and action of turning away from sin to God; in essence, turning our back on sin and the devil and looking at God face to face! As the scriptures clearly state when we behold the Lord with an open face we are changed into the same image (2 Corinthians 3:18). In order to be like Christ, we must see Him as He is, and that only continuously comes through repentance!

LESSON ELEVEN: THE WORD COVERING

As I was in prayer on November 30, 2016, praying in the Spirit, He showed me a vision. In the vision, there was a man covered by a large mantle with Hebrew writing on it. Then as God widened my view, I saw that there were several people both men and women underneath this great mantle. The Holy Ghost then spoke to me revealing that this large mantle was The Word of God covering those who had submitted themselves to its authority. He revealed to me that when we are covered by the Word, submitted to its authority, that His authority will literally rest UPON us. And the life of the Word will flow from within us (The Living Water of The Word) and He will be manifested.

The Word of God is only authoritative coming from us when we ourselves are submitted to its authority. That's what it means to speak words like Jesus. Words that are Spirit and Life; The words that we speak are from the Spirit and also being lived out within our own lives. This is the reason many preachers today do not operate in the power and authority they desire because they do not live what they preach. Yes, the word that most of them speak is spirit but it is not their lives. You see, we are made in the image of God and His Word is above His name. It should be the same with us; that His Word is above us. When Jesus died on the cross, the blood of the Living Word and the Living Water of the Word was released on the earth from His side for us, His Bride! St. John 19:34 says, ***"But one of the soldiers with a spear pierced his side, and forthwith came there out blood*** *and water.*" The scripture also says in St. John 1:14, *"And the Word was made flesh..."*

The blood that flowed from Jesus' (Living Word) veins was the eternal blood of the Word and the water was the Living water of the Word which flowed from His belly (St. John 7:38). That is one reason why the Bible calls Jesus the second Adam. Just as Adam went through surgery to bring forth His wife and bride; God took a rib from his side, likewise Jesus, when He was crucified was pierced in His side to bring forth His bride the Church. Jesus, the Living Word gave us our right to be reconciled by the shedding of His Blood on the cross.

The Bible says that our lives are hid in Him (Colossians 3:3) so in other words we are hid in the Word. Man relinquished his God-given authority when he through disobedience removed the covering of God's authoritative Word in the garden. No more did we have true authority in earth until Jesus came and sacrificed His life, The Word giving us His authority once again.

We must understand it's not just speaking the Word of God that gives us power. But it is the anointing of the Word that we speak that gives us power and that only comes through being submitted under the authority of the Word ourselves. We must be anointed to have the authority of His word. The scripture says that *"...hath made us kings and priests unto God and his Father; to him be glory and dominion forever and ever. Amen (Revelation 1:6)."*

To be kings (authority) and priests (relationship) we must be anointed by God. Only those who are anointed by God can wear the mantle of the Word. When we are covered (submitted) to the Word, the Word covers us with His authority. And only through the baptism of the Holy Spirit can we be truly anointed by God to wear the mantle of His Word! The Spirit of God is the life of the Word, so the life of the Word can't flow through us as He desires without being filled and anointed by the Holy Ghost. The scriptures say, *"But ye shall receive power, after that the Holy Ghost is come UPON you: and ye shall be witnesses unto me... (Acts 1:8)"*

For the Holy Spirit to come upon you is to mark you as Kingdom territory, hence the word King-dom; meaning the King's domain. If we are not the King's domain, we cannot operate under His delegated authority. It's simple: No Word, No Kingdom, No Kingdom, No power!

LESSON TWELVE: THE SEVEN SPIRITS OF GOD

This is one topic that really fascinated me when the Lord began to speak to me on this subject. I was always interested in the seven-fold manifestations of the Spirit. He is one Spirit, yet He manifests in seven different ways. The Lord led me through watching Christian television to read Isaiah 11:1-3 which reads, *"And there shall come forth a rod out of the stem of Jesse, and a Branch shall grow out of his roots: and the spirit of the Lord shall REST upon him, the spirit of WISDOM and UNDERSTANDING, the spirit of COUNSEL and MIGHT, the spirit of KNOWLEDGE and of the FEAR OF THE LORD; and shall make him of quick understanding in the fear of the Lord: and he shall not judge after the sight of the eyes, neither reprove after the hearing of the ears..."*

If the truth be told before this night of watching Christian television I didn't even know what the seven spirits of God were! So, this subject and revelation were brand new to me. I was also led to Revelations where the seven spirits of God are mentioned several times. One thing that stood out to me is that they are burning lamp stands before the Throne of God. They are lamps of fire because they provide light and reveal how the Church looks through each manifestation in the eyes of God the Father. I love how John in the first chapter of Revelation addresses and introduces the Holy Spirit as the *seven Spirits of God* when honoring the God's head. There are seven Spirits that make up the One Spirit of God, and we desperately need the manifestation of each Spirit in our churches. The Holy Ghost was sent to manifest Jesus, and these manifestations are parts of Him and of His life. Whatever Spirit we do not manifest is a part of Jesus that is not being seen in our churches.

The scripture says that we (the church) are to come into the measure of the stature of the fullness of Christ, and we can't do that if we are missing manifestations of His life or Spirit. All of these Spirits of God, the Father and The Lord Jesus want us to know intimately because they are Him. And not only does He want the church to know Him through the seven Spirits of God, but He wants the world to see Him through them, as a testimony that He is alive and risen from the dead! They are a part of our witness of Him. They make Him a reality to the sinner, and not just *a* reality, but *the* reality because of His supernatural power working in us. Often times without the anointing of conviction on the spoken Word of God, it is the power of God being made manifest that causes sinners to believe in Jesus as Lord and Savior. The Gospel and miracles, signs, and wonders go hand and hand. We should not have one without the other. But the power of God only comes through the Spirit of God as Zechariah 4:6 states, *"...Not by might, nor by power, but by my spirit, saith the Lord of Hosts."*

But before we can receive or be used to manifest the seven Spirits of God the Spirit must first *rest* on us, just as He did the Lord Jesus. For the Spirit to rest upon an individual He must not be resisted, but at a place of rest or peace with that individual. A place where that person is in willing submission to His will. He must first be able to rest on an individual to be made manifest the way that He was in the life of our Lord; and rest for the Holy Ghost requires obedience from those He resides with, in, and upon. When He is at rest so will you be at rest (peace) because He is the Lord of the Sabbath. Another point I want to bring out is in verse 3 of the eleventh chapter of Isaiah where he says that the Spirit shall make Him (Jesus) of quick understanding in the fear of the Lord.

There is a reason that the Spirit made (brought) Him to quick understanding in the fear of the Lord. It is because the fear of the Lord is the *beginning* of both wisdom and knowledge, and the foundation along with repentance for revelation. To fear the Lord is *not* to be scared of God, how can you build an intimate relationship with someone you're scared of? 1 John 4:18 says, *"There is no fear in love; but perfect love casteth out fear: because fear hath torment. He that feareth is not made perfect in love.*

The fear of the Lord as I learned from international Christian author and teacher John Bevere is *to be terrified to be away from the Lord.* When we truly realize to be separated from God is the greatest tragedy that one can experience, then we have begun on the path in the fear of the Lord. If we think about it, that's what hell is, eternal separation from God! The fire, the torment, the violent presence of billions of demons, believe it or not it is not the worst part of hell. It is being eternally separated from everything that is truly Good and that is God.

As the scripture says in the first chapter of James *every* good and perfect gift is from above and comes from God. Every good thing in life that we experience from the sound of birds chirping in the morning, time with loved ones, to an evening sunset, *all come from God!* In Exodus 20:20 it reads, **"And Moses said unto the people, Fear not: for God is come to prove you, and that his fear may be before your faces, that ye sin not. And the people stood afar off, and Moses drew near unto the thick darkness where God was."** You see, the Lord told the people of Israel to *fear not,* that He came to prove them and that His fear would be before their faces. He didn't want them to be scared of Him; He wanted them to draw near to Him, just as Moses did! The fear of the Lord is to fear being separated from Him, *not* the other way around. In His Presence is the absence of sin, that's why He said that His fear may be before their faces so they would not sin. Anyone who constantly dwells in the manifest presence of God will be *much less* likely to sin. As James said in the first chapter of his letter, **"But every man is tempted, when he is drawn away of his own lust, and enticed (James 1:14)."** So, it is important for us as saints to be of quick understanding in the fear of the Lord, because it not only draws us close to The Lord, but it sanctifies our lives. As Solomon wrote, **"By mercy and truth iniquity is purged: and by the fear of the Lord men depart from evil (Proverbs 16:6)."**

LESSON THIRTEEN: THE GIFTS OF THE SPIRIT

It is essential for the last-day church of Jesus Christ to be equipped and skillful in the gifts that the Spirit has given to us as our spiritual heritage. Especially when we consider that we are in a vicious battle with a supernatural kingdom of darkness.

So it is for the saints, as 2 Corinthians 10:4 states *"For the weapons of our warfare are not carnal, but mighty through God..."*

But for us as saints to be effective in warfare and in bringing many souls to Christ we must be skillful with our weapons!

Our Apostle Paul so emphatically wrote *TWO* crucial statements as he was inspired by the Holy Ghost. The first being: *"Now concerning spiritual gifts, brethren, I would NOT have you IGNORANT (1 Corinthians 12:1)"* and the second being: *"But COVET EARNESTLY the BEST gifts... (1 Corinthians 12:31)."*

The first statement let us know that we as saints can be *ignorant* of the gifts of the Spirit, and if we are ignorant of something, that means we don't know how it works, how to function in it, or if we have them. And if we do, how to recognize what gift it is.

To put the second statement in perspective, nowhere else in scripture are we instructed or commanded by God to covet anything, except *the **gifts of*** *the Spirit!*

The gifts of the Spirit (**1 Corinthians 12:8-10**) are given in 3 categories: gifts of **revelation,** gifts of **power,** and gifts of **inspiration.**

- **Gifts of Revelation** — the word of wisdom, the word of knowledge, and discerning of spirits.

- **Gifts of Power** — the gift of faith, the gifts of healing, and the gift of miracles.

- **Gifts of Inspiration** — the gift of prophecy, the gift of diverse tongues, and the gift of interpretation of tongues *(This group of gifts are given specifically for the Church).*

GIFTS OF REVELATION

- The Word of Wisdom — a supernatural revelation from God of His mind and purpose (foretelling the future).

There are many examples of the operation of the word of wisdom in scripture, every true prophet in the Bible possessed this gift (which is insight into the mind and purpose of God or in other words to see and/or know the future through the revelation of the Spirit.) This gift is often referred to as prophecy in the scripture!

- The Word of Knowledge — a supernatural revelation from God of any fact or event.

Examples of the word of knowledge are: 1 Kings 19:18 when Elijah thought that he was the last prophet of God in Israel and God gave him a word of Knowledge (supernatural revelation of fact) that He still had 7,000 prophets in Israel who had not bowed to Baal.

Another example of the word of knowledge is in St. John 4 when Jesus meets the women at the well and revealed to her supernaturally through the Holy Ghost facts about her life (such as having five husbands) and she immediately became an evangelist for Christ bringing a whole city to Him, because of the operation of this gift!

The Discerning of spirits — a supernatural revelation from God of the presence or activity of the spirit realm.

An example of this gift is when Elisha discerned the spirits of angels on chariots of fire encamped all around them and prayed that the Lord would open his servant's eyes to see as well.

*This is a cleansing gift (because it reveals the hidden intents of heart and spirit) and a gift of protection given to church to help present it without spot or wrinkle to The Master!

GIFTS OF POWER

- The Gift of Faith — a supernatural power given by God, protecting from harm or danger.

A great example of the operation of this gift is Daniel in the Lion's Den. God imparted to Daniel supernatural faith to go into the Lion's den and rest, knowing that He would be preserved (which we know is naturally impossible).

Another example of this gift would be when Moses by The Spirit was given supernatural faith to drop his staff and watch God transform it into a snake and consume the sorcerer's snakes and transform back into his staff.

*This gift is God supernaturally acting on our behalf apart from any effort by us.

- The Gift of Miracles — a supernatural power producing signs and wonders.

Examples of this gift are shown all throughout Scripture, but some examples would be Moses splitting the red sea, Elijah calling fire down from Heaven, Joshua stopping the sun, and the Apostles casting out demons and devils and raising men and women from the dead.

*This gift is God supernaturally working through us.

- The Gifts of Healing — a supernatural power given by God removing disease and infirmity.

You can find examples of healing all throughout the New Testament;

healing from leprosy, blindness, deafness, and lame body parts, etc.

*These gifts are given often for specific diseases and infirmities to certain individuals for physical healing of the body.

GIFTS OF INSPIRATION

- <u>The Gift of Prophecy</u> — a supernatural utterance inspired by God, in a known tongue.

Examples of this gift can be seen all throughout the Psalms and most of both the Old and New Testament Scripture are a result of this gift being in operation (Spirit inspired utterances of edification, exhortation, and comfort)

This gift is often confused with the word of wisdom (foretelling the future). Many times in the scripture when it's says that men and women began to prophecy they weren't telling the future, but speaking under the Spirit's inspiration words of edification, exhortation and comfort (1 Corinthians 14:3).

*This gift could be called the poetry of the Spirit and is often the gift in operation when anointed songs are given (written) to men by The Spirit of God, hence the Psalms!

- <u>The Gift of Divers Kinds of Tongues</u> — a supernatural utterance inspired by God, in an unknown tongue.

We do not see an example of this gift in operation in the Scripture, but it is spoken about in 1 Corinthians 14 by the Apostle Paul, this gift and the gift of interpretation of tongues equal prophecy.

*This gift is a Spirit inspired message of edification, exhortation, and comfort in an unknown tongue (except by a person from that nation or fluent in that language that hears the message).

- <u>The Gift of Interpretation</u> — a supernatural utterance inspired by God, interpreting an unknown tongue.

Once again we do not see this gift in operation in Scripture but is spoken of by the Apostle Paul in 1 Corinthians 14.

*This gift is the interpretation (not translation) of tongues. The message

of God may take the believer who is under the anointing of the Spirit three minutes to deliver in an unknown tongue; but the interpreter of the tongues 30 seconds to interpret. It is not a word for word translation from the Spirit, but a main point (heart of the message) translation from the Holy Ghost through a believer.

LESSON FOURTEEN: THE GATHERING

There is something very important that every believer on the face of the Earth must know and understand. It is the gathering or the great harvest that is going to take place before the rapture of the Church. You see, before Christ can rapture or catch away His Church (Bride), she must be glorious without spot or wrinkle or any such thing. And anyone with eyes can see that the Church at large is *not* that. So, there must be a cleansing judgement within the body of Christ to prepare us for our magnificent King, who is worthy of a beautiful bride. The Scripture says, ***"For the time is come that judgement must begin at the house of God: and if it first begin at us, what shall be the end of them that obey not the gospel of God? (1 Peter 4:17)."***

God is now in the process of increasingly judging His house, so that His house will not be condemned with the world. He is shaking His Church, and anything that is not founded on the sure foundation of Jesus Christ will fall. Some of us have built our faith on our local assemblies, certain truths, organizations, denominations, etc., but none of those things will stand in this ever-increasing judgement of God on His house, only those who are built upon Jesus will stand! We must understand that the judgement of God is not fire and lightening from heaven, but it is God causing His people to agree with Him, and to see as He sees. Whether we know it or not most of our views of God are distorted and unbalanced, mine included. But we are only changed as we see Him as He is with open face, by the Spirit of God (**2 Corinthians 3:18**). We must become a Christ-centered Church, not denomination centered, not organization centered, not even ministry centered but *Jesus Christ centered!*

The Holy Ghost spoke to me prophetically in 2012, He said, *"We are entering and are now in a season of separation, the wheat from the tares, the children of light from the children of darkness, the children of God from the children of satan, and men's hearts are going to be revealed, so that the people of God may know who labors among them and can become the people of God He is calling for in these last and evil days."* God is now beginning the separation spoken of in Matthew 13. As time moves on it will become blatantly obvious who is of God and who's not, there will be no gray area. Men's hearts *will* be revealed whether good or bad, because of the increase of the manifest Presence of God in the Church and on the Earth. But we have to soberly understand that wrath (punishment) will come much quicker and harshly in the manifest Presence of God. Because God shows more mercy where He is the least revealed, but where He is clearly seen or revealed, He is much less tolerant of sin! Ask Ananias and Sapphira in Acts 5, what happens when you willfully sin in the manifest Presence of God. There must once again come a holy reverence and fear of the Lord in His house. Only then can we receive the purest revelation of God that has yet to be seen on Earth, and it *will happen!*

The Scripture in Psalms 19 says that the fear of the Lord is clean enduring *forever.* It is the fear of the Lord that helps purify the life of a believer and builds an everlasting foundation of relationship between them and The Lord. The fear of the Lord is the *beginning of knowledge.* It is the fear of the Lord that begins your experiential knowledge of The Lord or is the beginning of being close to Him. It is the fear of the Lord that causes a believer to depart from evil (**Proverbs 16:6**). Only those who fear the Lord can come and abide before His Throne for eternity, *no one* who doesn't fear Him will be in Heaven before His Throne! God is holy! And everyone who dwells with Him forever will be also.

He wants to dwell among His people, not just visit, but *dwell.* But He will only dwell with those who are able or who have prepared themselves to live constantly in His presence. Our God is a consuming fire and all wood, hay, and stubble which are acts of the flesh will be consumed in His manifest Presence. Only that which is gold, silver, and precious stone (Kingdom acts) can last and be purified in His Presence. As 1 Corinthians 3:11-15, *"For other foundation can no man lay than that is laid, which is Jesus Christ. Now if any man build upon this foundation gold, silver, precious stones, wood, hay, stubble; Every man's work shall be made manifest: for the day shall declare it, because it shall be revealed by fire; and the fire shall try every man's work of what sort it is. If any man's work abide which he hath built thereupon, he shall receive a reward. If any man's work shall be burned, he shall suffer loss: but he himself shall be saved."*

I don't know about you, but I do not want to suffer loss before the Lord. I want to have a reward and a life that was fruitful and pleasing to Him. To be faithful in the eyes of God as a servant or steward we must multiply what He has given us, only then can He trust us with more. In order for this great gathering to take place (and has already begun in different parts of the world) the saints must get into shape and place. The saints must spiritually condition themselves for harvest because harvest is work. But if we are used to being lazy Christians or just bench warmers so to speak, we will not be in shape for the great harvest that God is bringing in. We must also be in place, we must find our callings, gifts, operations, and offices and function in them. That is the *only* way that we can be as the scripture says, "fitly joined together." But all these things are ordained and given by The Spirit of God, and we must diligently seek Him to know our place in Him. It is *not* where we want to be, but where we are called to be (which will often be where you're least comfortable). For the simple fact that it causes you to totally lean and depend on Him for grace (power) to do the work He has called you to do and helps us stay humble before Him and others.

In these last hours God is going to pour more grace on the church than has ever been seen before, even by the apostles! But only upon those who have prepared themselves to be laborers in the harvest. Many in the church will actually be a part of the harvest or being gathered in, instead of laborers in the harvest. This will happen for many reasons and at the same time one reason: because our foundation is not built on Jesus alone. We the church of the Most High God must learn to live in the spirit realm and not just visit from time to time. If we love God (who is a Spirit) and want to be with Him than we must dwell in the Spirit. Those who learn to dwell in the Spirit or in His Presence constantly will be entrusted with the last day oil and power, power which will be unparalleled. One reason the power of God will be so great is because evil will be so great, both the Light and the darkness will come to full maturity in the earth. All that has been sown into the world in both good and evil will be reaped in this generation.

Isaiah 60:1-5 speaks about this great harvest of souls, *"Arise, shine; for thy light is come, and the glory of the Lord is risen upon thee. For, behold, the darkness shall cover the earth, and gross darkness the people: but the Lord shall arise upon thee, and his glory shall be seen upon thee. And the gentiles shall come to thy light, and kings to the brightness of thy rising. Lift up thine eyes round about, and see: all they gather themselves together, they come to thee: thy sons shall come from far, and thy daughters shall be nursed at thy side. Then thou shalt see, and flow together, and thine heart shall fear, and be enlarged; because of the abundance of the sea(people) shall be converted unto thee, the forces of the Gentiles shall come to thee."* We are coming into the most glorious days to be a Christian, true disciples of Jesus Christ. The latter will be greater than the former, Jesus Christ will be seen like never before, **LITERALLY!** He will be physically manifesting in services, to groups of believers and individuals as He did in the Bible but to a much greater degree. The appearances of angels will become common among believers and to the world, the Kingdom of God will literally invade the earth. Children will move mightily in the Spirit casting out devils, teenagers will be some of the greatest preachers of the Gospel the world has ever seen (In the last days your sons and daughters shall prophecy). They will lay hands on hospitals and everyone in the hospital will be healed, they will empty psych wards because of the power of God. Mighty apostles and prophets will be followed by the news like celebrities, to see the move of God by their hands and words. There will literally be thousands like Paul, Peter, John, John the Baptist and the others, they will be called the messengers of power!

The church will once again be the city on a hill that *cannot be hid!* Entire cities and regions will be changed by one message of the Gospel being preached just like with Jonah in the Bible. Cities will literally for seasons have zero crime in them because of the glory and governing of the Holy Ghost. The people of God will stop the rain from falling, even call fire down from Heaven. Devout satanists will be converted by mighty evangelists invading the enemy's territory preaching the Gospel. There will be places where the Power of God is so strong that anyone with ill intentions will not be able to enter or fall dead trying. Many will see angelic camps around churches and refuges of Christians protecting them, and many of the enemies of the church will flee. The manifest glory of God will be on some just like it was on Moses when he had to wear a vail over his face coming from the mountain of God. God will become reality to the world, He will be as real as the ground they walk on. He will be so literally manifested that those who reject Him will be openly doing so in full knowledge of His reality. This is the reason that the wrath of God will be so great, because of open rejection.

The Holy Ghost spoke a Word to me one Sunday morning before going to service, *"All men need a Savior, and they will choose one in the coming days, the days will be so bad, that they will have to look to someone else, some higher power, but if they do not know the True Savior, they will settle and believe in the counterfeit, that demonic prince anti-Christ."* If we do not know Jesus personally which begins with repentance and faith in His work on the Cross and His resurrection, which results in the new birth (born again) or being born of the Spirit, we *will fall* for the deception of the anti-Christ. The only power that can keep you from this deception is the Blood of Jesus and the sealing of The Holy Spirit! The best and worst times to ever hit the earth are unfolding in our day, your *relationship* with Jesus will determine which side you will be on! Even in having a relationship with Jesus, how deep or intimate our relationship is will determine the magnitude of glory that will be in and on our lives. So, grow close to Jesus through the Person of The Holy Spirit and allow Him to equip and prepare you for the greatest spiritual battle and harvest the world has ever seen! I also received a word of wisdom from Jesus on this matter, He said to me, *"There is a battle coming that My people are not prepared for, that will precede My coming, tell them that they must be so in tune with My Spirit in order to be equipped and able to gain victory."*

It is the Holy Spirit that keeps us on the path to life and we must hear and follow Him, regardless of what the world is doing. And do not be alarmed when this move of God comes into full swing, when many dry and institutionalized Christians resist this *supernatural move* of God. Those who don't believe in the supernatural happening in our times or the functioning of the gifts of the Spirit in our times, those who believe in the God of yesterday and forget today and forevermore! They will honestly believe that they are doing God service and preserving the true faith but will actually be resisting the Holy Spirit. Many of them will turn to God in a new way, when they see the power of God manifested in their own lives whether through miracles or judgement. These will be amazing times for the people of God, contrary to what many are saying. I learned from Prophet Hank Kunneman that many are prophesying doom and gloom in these last days but that is because they are only seeing from the second heaven, which is where Satan and his demonic host dwell in the mid-air. So, all they see is the strategy and attacks of the enemy but have not elevated their spirit to prophesy from the third Heaven where the Almighty reigns supreme! And to receive insight and revelation into the miraculous things that God is doing and has in store for His last-day saints!

Now we do have to understand that with mighty moves of God also comes persecution, they pretty much go hand in hand. Because the Kingdom of God will be so mightily manifested so will the kingdom of darkness. You see, Satan can't not stop the glory of God so his desire is to stop or kill the ones the glory is on. But realize this eternal truth, that it is the greatest honor in Heaven to be a martyr for the Lord Jesus Christ! This should not be a fear or torment but an *honor* in the hearts in minds of every believer to die for their Master. But not all will be martyrs many will last until the day of the rapture being caught up and changed in the mid-air to be like Jesus! But only the Church without spot, or wrinkle or any such thing will be caught up, the lukewarm church will be left behind and have to endure the Great Tribulation and eventually become martyrs in order to enter into the Kingdom of Heaven, because your love and faithfulness to Jesus must be proven.

CONCLUSION

I truly pray that this Spirit inspired book has been an edifying blessing to you. That you have been both challenged and enlightened. I hope that this book will be a source to help you bear much fruit in the kingdom of God and to ultimately cultivate a more intimate relationship with the Person of the Holy Spirit.

"He that hath an ear, let him hear what the Spirit saith unto the churches (Revelations 3:22)."

ABOUT THE AUTHOR

Paige Michael Williams is a minister of the Gospel of Jesus Christ from northeast Ohio. God speaks to him by revelation through dreams and visions, as well as prophetically. In 2017 He was given a commission by The Lord to "Write down what you hear." This book is just a small fulfillment of that commission.

Seraph Creative is a collective of artists, writers, theologians & illustrators who desire to see the body of Christ grow into full maturity, walking in their inheritance as Sons of God on the Earth.

Sign up to our newsletter to know about future exciting releases.

Visit our website :

www.seraphcreative.org